*GREATER THAN
 ALSO AVAIL
    AUDIOBOOK FORMAT.

Greater Than a Tourist Book Series Reviews from Readers

I think the series is wonderful and beneficial for tourists to get information before visiting the city.

-Seckin Zumbul, Izmir Turkey

I am a world traveler who has read many trip guides but this one really made a difference for me. I would call it a heartfelt creation of a local guide expert instead of just a guide.

-Susy, Isla Holbox, Mexico

New to the area like me, this is a must have!

 -Joe, Bloomington, USA

This is a good series that gets down to it when looking for things to do at your destination without having to read a novel for just a few ideas.

-Rachel, Monterey, USA

Good information to have to plan my trip to this destination.

-Pennie Farrell, Mexico

Great ideas for a port day.

-Mary Martin USA

Aptly titled, you won't just be a tourist after reading this book. You'll be greater than a tourist!

-Alan Warner, Grand Rapids, USA

Even though I only have three days to spend in San Miguel in an upcoming visit, I will use the author's suggestions to guide some of my time there. An easy read - with chapters named to guide me in directions I want to go.

-Robert Catapano, USA

Great insights from a local perspective! Useful information and a very good value!

-Sarah, USA

This series provides an in-depth experience through the eyes of a local. Reading these series will help you to travel the city in with confidence and it'll make your journey a unique one.

-Andrew Teoh, Ipoh, Malaysia

>TOURIST

GREATER THAN A TOURIST- MAUI HAWAII USA

50 Travel Tips from a Local

Skye Anderson

Greater Than a Tourist-Maui Hawaii USA Copyright © 2021 by CZYK Publishing LLC. All Rights Reserved.

All rights reserved. No part of this book may be reproduced in any form or by any electronic or mechanical means including information storage and retrieval systems, without permission in writing from the author. The only exception is by a reviewer, who may quote short excerpts in a review.

The statements in this book are of the authors and may not be the views of CZYK Publishing or Greater Than a Tourist.
First Edition
Cover designed by: Ivana Stamenkovic
Cover Image: https://pixabay.com/photos/beach-resort-hawaii-maui-vacation-174561/

Image 1: By Jawed Karim - Own work, CC BY-SA 3.0, https://commons.wikimedia.org/w/index.php?curid=32416584
Image 2: By dronepicr - Westküste Maui Hawaii, CC BY 2.0, https://commons.wikimedia.org/w/index.php?curid=74172759
Image 3: By dronepicr - Makena Beach, Maui Hawaii, CC BY 2.0, https://commons.wikimedia.org/w/index.php?curid=74172961
Image 4: By dronepicr - Waianapanapa State Park Maui Hawaii Road to Hana, CC BY 2.0, https://commons.wikimedia.org/w/index.php?curid=74172471

CZYK Publishing Since 2011.
CZYKPublishing.com
Greater Than a Tourist

Lock Haven, PA
All rights reserved.
ISBN: 9798509477119

>TOURIST

>TOURIST
50 TRAVEL TIPS FROM A LOCAL

>TOURIST

BOOK DESCRIPTION

With travel tips and culture in our guidebooks written by a local, it is never too late to visit Maui. Greater Than a Tourist- Maui Hawaii United States by Author Skye Anderson offers the inside scoop on Maui Hawaii, The Valley Isle. Most travel books tell you how to travel like a tourist. Although there is nothing wrong with that, as part of the 'Greater Than a Tourist' series, this book will give you candid travel tips from someone who has lived at your next travel destination. This guide book will not tell you exact addresses or store hours but instead gives you knowledge that you may not find in other smaller print travel books. Experience cultural, culinary delights, and attractions with the guidance of a Local. Slow down and get to know the people with this invaluable guide. By the time you finish this book, you will be eager and prepared to discover new activities at your next travel destination.

Inside this travel guide book you will find:

Visitor information from a Local
Tour ideas and inspiration
Save time with valuable guidebook information

Greater Than a Tourist- A Travel Guidebook with 50 Travel Tips from a Local. Slow down, stay in one place, and get to know the people and culture. By the time you finish this book, you will be eager and prepared to travel to your next destination.

>TOURIST

OUR STORY

Traveling is a passion of the Greater than a Tourist book series creator. Lisa studied abroad in college, and for their honeymoon Lisa and her husband toured Europe. During her travels to Malta, an older man tried to give her some advice based on his own experience living on the island since he was a young boy. She was not sure if she should talk to the stranger but was interested in his advice. When traveling to some places she was wary to talk to locals because she was afraid that they weren't being genuine. Through her travels, Lisa learned how much locals had to share with tourists. Lisa created the Greater Than a Tourist book series to help connect people with locals. A topic that locals are very passionate about sharing.

TABLE OF CONTENTS

Book Description
Our Story
Table of Contents
Dedication
About the Author
How to Use This Book
From the Publisher
WELCOME TO > TOURIST
1. TRY THE LOCAL FOOD
2. FOOD IS EXPENSIVE
3. AVOID CHAIN RESTAURANTS
4. TRY ALL THE FRUIT
5. TRYING TO DEPART WITH FRUITS OR PLANTS
6. PACK JUST THE ESSENTIALS
7. TIME-ZONE
8. ECO - FRIENDLY SUNSCREEN
9. RESEARCH YOUR BEACHES
10. HITCH-HIKING IS A THING HERE
11. CONSTANTLY CHECK THE WEATHER
12. EVERY PART OF THE ISLAND HAS A SLIGHTLY DIFFERENT WEATHER PATTERN
13. BRING WARM CLOTHES

14. PICK THE RIGHT TIME OF YEAR TO TRAVEL
15. FIND THE RIGHT LUAU
16. CONSIDER PACKING YOUR OWN SNORKEL GEAR
17. FOOTWEAR
18. PACK A FIRST AID KIT
19. PLANT LIFE
20. LOCK YOUR CAR DOORS
21. FIND A GOOD PAIR OF SHADES
22. DO NOT TOUCH THE SEA TURTLES
23. NOT ALL RESIDENTS ARE "HAWAIIAN"
24. CHOOSE YOUR NEXT ISLAND FROM HERE
25. ISLAND TIME IS A REAL THING
26. DO NOT IGNORE WARNING SIGNS
27. PICK THE RIGHT TIME OF YEAR TO TRAVEL
28. WHALE WATCHING IS NOT YEAR - ROUND
29. DON'T JUST STAY IN RESORT TOWNS
30. LEAVE THE CHICKENS ALONE
31. LOCAL ARTISTS
32. CHECK OUT THE LOCAL ART GALLERIES
33. FIND A DRUM CIRCLE
34. THE ROAD TO HANA
35. BAMBOO FOREST

36. DON'T MISS OUT ON HALEAKALA
37. GUIDED BIKE TOUR DOWN HALEAKALA
38. DO NOT TAKE LAVA ROCKS
39. FIND A ZIPLINE
40. VISIT THE LAHAINA BANYAN TREE
41. BRING CASH BEFORE DEPARTING
42. NAKALELE POINT BLOWHOLE
43. IAO VALLEY
44. WATCH OUT FOR CENTIPEDES
45. PACKAGE DEALS
46. GROCERY BAGS
47. BRING A LITTLE SOMETHING
48. GRATUITIES
49. TAKE YOUR SHOES OFF BEFORE ENTERING
50. PACK IT IN PACK IT OUT

TOP REASONS TO BOOK THIS TRIP

Packing and Planning Tips

Travel Questions

Travel Bucket List

NOTES

\>TOURIST

DEDICATION

This book is dedicated to Cedar Nieland, for always motivating me that there is more in life, and always adventure awaiting!

ABOUT THE AUTHOR

Skye is a mother of one. She lives in Billings, Montana loves to snowboard with her family, spend every moment outdoors and she loves to travel…

\>TOURIST

HOW TO USE THIS BOOK

The *Greater Than a Tourist* book series was written by someone who has lived in an area for over three months. The goal of this book is to help travelers either dream or experience different locations by providing opinions from a local. The author has made suggestions based on their own experiences. Please check before traveling to the area in case the suggested places are unavailable.

Travel Advisories: As a first step in planning any trip abroad, check the Travel Advisories for your intended destination.
https://travel.state.gov/content/travel/en/traveladvisories/traveladvisories.html

FROM THE PUBLISHER

Traveling can be one of the most important parts of a person's life. The anticipation and memories that you have are some of the best. As a publisher of the Greater Than a Tourist, as well as the popular *50 Things to Know* book series, we strive to help you learn about new places, spark your imagination, and inspire you. Wherever you are and whatever you do I wish you safe, fun, and inspiring travel.

Lisa Rusczyk Ed. D.
CZYK Publishing

>TOURIST

```
WELCOME TO
> TOURIST
```

>TOURIST

Volcanic rocks protrude on a Maui beach

West Coast of Maui

Makena Beach, South Maui

Waianapanapa State Park in East Maui, next to Hana

>TOURIST

*"And into the forest I go, to lose
my mind and find my soul"*

- John Muir

Maui was my first "away from home" travel experience. Growing up in a small town in northern Idaho, I was full of anticipation and desire about what the world was about… When I was eighteen I took the ground running and hopped on a plane with my best friend. Little did I know I was embarking on a journey that was going to not only change my life forever, but help me realize my true love for travel.

From the few years I spent living in Maui, Hawaii, I got to fully experience what "Island Life" was really about. Growing up I dreamed about travel. I dreamed of experiencing all the beauty and culture this world of ours has to offer. Only, when I dreamed of this, I imagined myself learning and educating myself about the diversity in lifestyles. I wanted to know what it was like to LIVE there, not just visit. I have moved around dozens of times in my life already, spending 1-2 years at a time in each place, to really absorb the environment and area I was living in. And to be entirely honest...from my experience, when you live in a high-profile tourist area, tourism can play a huge role in the economy for all the money it brings in. However, there are also locals that are not the most fond of tourists, due to past experiences of people ruining it for the rest of us and giving tourists a bad rap. This is why I always reiterate two very important things, as much as I can to those traveling.

ALWAYS BE RESPECTFUL… because you are a visitor, and that is not your home.

SUPPORT LOCAL as much as you can.

Inside this guide, you will find tips that I have learned from living in Maui and getting to know the locals, and their lifestyle. Maui is one to truly be appreciated and respected, because it is a magical place. Treat the land with respect, and it will do the same for you. Enjoy!

>TOURIST

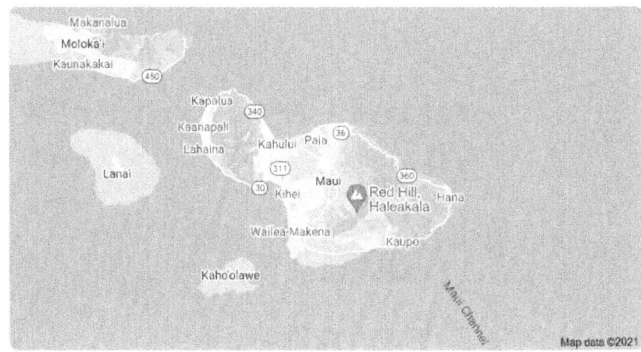

Maui
Hawaii, USA

Maui Hawaii Climate

	High	Low
January	71	55
February	70	55
March	71	55
April	73	56
May	74	57
June	76	59
July	77	60
August	78	61
September	77	60
October	77	60
November	74	58
December	72	56

GreaterThanaTourist.com

Temperatures are in Fahrenheit degrees.
Source: climate-data.org

>TOURIST

1. TRY THE LOCAL FOOD

This is by far my favorite tip, because I don't know about you but I love trying new foods! Which is why I put it at the very top of the list. I saw so many people visiting Maui and STILL go to Mcdonalds, Dennys, Burger King or some other chain restaurant they probably swing through once a week back home. What's fun in that!? I can understand, sometimes going to a new place is overwhelming and you do not know where exactly the good places to get food are. That is what these wonderful travel tips are for! Hawaii is full of all sorts of odds and ends cultural food options. Even stopping by the gas station to grab snacks, you will always find one of my favorites...Spam Musubi, it is usually in the deli area. Many people are turned away from the idea of spam, but honestly unless you have tried it and concretely decided you don't like it, you're missing out on a fun experience. I bashed spam for almost a year before I tried it! I was then kicking myself because it became my go to snack on the way to work. One food that I fell in love with (to my own surprise actually) was poke and poke bowls (which is tuna). I have always loved sushi, but the idea of eating ONLY raw fish I was a little weary about. To be honest though, you are on an island...if you are going to get fresh delicious fish anywhere, it is here! Plus, there are a bunch of different seasoned versions of poke to try before you just rule it out, because this is definitely an island fave, people also get turned away thinking you have to go to a fancy restaurant or to a resort to get the full experience, but this is not true at all. The best places to find great food here are the little 'hole in the wall' spots! That tiny little diner that caught your eye on the corner or food trucks along the roadside! These are the places where you will find wonderful food made with lots of culture and love! My suggestion… eat as much fish as you can! If you are not the biggest fan of fish, put kalua pork on your list of foods to try. Most pizza places offer a kalua pork pineapple barbeque pizza that will melt in your mouth and have you trying to recreate it back home! Get out of your comfort zone here, I promise it will be well worth it!

>TOURIST

2. FOOD IS EXPENSIVE

Shipping costs to get food to the island is expensive for businesses, therefore they have to upcharge (understandably, how else would they stay afloat?) but there are ways around it. For instance when doing a day trip to a waterfall or hiking through the bamboo forest, opt for snacks and lunch items from a local market instead of going out to eat every time. One thing I always loved about the supermarkets there, is that the deli always offers GREAT grab-n-go options! This is where you could try that delicious poke I spoke of earlier. There are also usually fresh made sandwiches, and plenty of choices you can pack in a cooler for a nice picnic! The "deli" food on the island is much different than what you would find in a deli back home. It is always fresh, and always authentic. Plus this way you can experience the lifestyle and food and save a few bucks!

3. AVOID CHAIN RESTAURANTS

There are Denny's, Mcdonalds, Taco Bell, Wendy's, IHOP, and most chain restaurants in Maui, and as tempting as it is to swing through the drive-thru right after landing for a quick pick me up, I would refrain. I know for some people stepping out of your comfort zone can be a challenge, but that is what Travel is all about! Experiencing something new, trying and seeing new things. If you are starving from the long flight and need a quick meal, instead of hitting a chain restaurant, go through a local drive thru! "L & L Drive Inn" located in Kahului (the town you will fly into) is a great fast option for hawaiian plate lunches. There are plenty of choices for quick drive-thru food that you wouldn't be able to try just any other day.

I will admit, I went to a Denny's while I lived in Maui, the first week of living there, and honestly it wasn't a terrible experience because it is much different than Denny's on the mainland. There are no windows so it is completely open, and there are little birds flying around and landing on the floor next to you picking up little crumbs. Adorable right!? That was my first realization of just how 'lax' the lifestyle

>TOURIST

is there!wThe food though.... was nothing to write about. The experience was neat seeing the difference from a Denny's on the mainland, but looking back on it I would have absolutely chosen to check out a local food restaurant instead. You are on one of the most beautiful islands in the world and the food matches the scenery! Get out of your comfort zone and go find a local restaurant, It will be well worth it! 10 minute drive to northshore town, Paia there is a restaurant in the center of town called Paia Fishmarket... GREAT fish tacos!

4. TRY ALL THE FRUIT

I cannot express this enough, TRY ALL THE FRUIT YOU CAN POSSIBLY HANDLE! After living on Maui for so many years, one of the hardest parts about returning to the mainland was not being able to eat all the fruit the island has to offer! I am dead serious when I say I had dreams of just eating pineapple on the beach. All of the fruit there is very large and very aromatic, I would definitely suggest checking out a local market and stocking up on fruit to try throughout your trip, take some back to the hotel, and to just have on hand for snacks.

There is "passion fruit" which is called "lilikoi" in hawaiian, guava, strawberry guava, star fruit, jackfruit, and so many others that I suggest trying. I am not kidding when I say TRY EVERYTHING!

One thing to keep in mind is that much of the fruit grows all over the island, so you may find mangos or avocado that have fallen from a tree. I wouldn't suggest picking them up to eat because depending on how far they fell from the tree they may be fairly bruised, and after not too long of being on the ground the bugs will get to them. Most importantly though you want to make sure it is not on someone's private property. You may also find coconuts along the road side when driving and these can be a great score! However coconuts are difficult to open if you do not have the correct utensils. There are coconut openers that you can buy at most grocery stores that are shaped like a T with a point which are pretty handy, or you can ask a local if they could open it for you (most probably carry one in their vehicle or at least have a machete - and yes you can open a coconut with a machete, very easily actually and it is quite fun to watch!) Just whatever you do… do not try to open a coconut by hitting it on a rock or a hard object. Believe it or not, I have seen it before and it is hilarious, and you will most likely be laughed at.

>TOURIST

5. TRYING TO DEPART WITH FRUITS OR PLANTS

When the sad moment came, and I was leaving the hawaiian islands, one thing I really wanted to bring back home was an avocado seed! I was informed very quickly that there are actually very strict regulations on departing with actually any type of vegetation, period. Because just one piece of fruit or a plant can contain certain contaminants such as an invasive pest or disease that could be harbored, and this means to or from Maui. Maui is also a rabies free state, which is why it is such a time-consuming mission to bring a pet over to the island. They do everything they can to contain the sanctity of the island. So keep that in mind!

6. PACK JUST THE ESSENTIALS

When it comes to packing, I know many go way overboard, especially the ladies. I say this, because I am an overpacker. Always. You never know the occasion may be so why not just bring it all right?

Well when it comes to packing, you really need to keep in mind WHAT you will be doing, and go from there. Always plan your trip completely before you pack, because there are a few items you could actually bring with you that could save you some serious bucks! Swimsuits are the most commonly forgotten item when traveling here, and for that reason there are loads of 'Window Shops' selling absolutely adorable swimsuits, but you will be dropping some serious cash so make a checklist!

7. TIME-ZONE

Depending on where you are departing from you will want to keep in mind the time zone difference when you are choosing a flight. Departing from SEATTLE, WA I was not looking at too bad of a time change, even then I found that the time zone still slightly messed with my sleep and energy levels. For those flying from a farther distance can get some serious jet-lag... and when you arrive in Maui and take those first steps out of the airport smelling that first smell of flowery, humid air... you do not want to have to go straight to the hotel and take a nap because you are zonked from the flight. Pack plenty of entertainment and snacks for the plane ride, but also pack a nice pillow, because you are flying directly over the ocean the majority of the time so it can seem like it is longer than it is.

8. ECO - FRIENDLY SUNSCREEN

Majority of the commonly used sunscreens today contain quite a few hard chemicals that are not the best for your body, but they are also terrible for the environment. This is huge over on the island because once you get into the ocean, any remaining product on your skin gets into the water and affects the coral reefs and overall ocean life. This can be lotion or perfume, but the most common is sunscreen. It may seem hard to find an eco-friendly sunscreen before departing for your trip, but this is an item I actually suggest getting once you arrive on the island, as Maui actually offers many eco-friendly sunscreen options. You don't want to be that person that is standing in the water and you have a ring of oil looking substance around you, you may not get the best looks from locals, polluting their waters!

9. RESEARCH YOUR BEACHES

Most beaches in Maui are open to the public. There are some beaches however that are public but may have connected sections that are not public. For example if you started to notice the beach connecting to a property with a beach house on it, you may have wandered to a private section. These are usually posted with signs making it very clear though, so just make sure you are paying attention to that.

There are also a select few beaches that are actually nude beaches, and these are usually smaller and do not have a direct access point, but if you are meandering around they may be very easy to come across by accident. Doing research will not necessarily help you to avoid or find these beaches,

>TOURIST

but knowing to keep an eye open will help you on your trip. Now if you are on your honeymoon with your significant other, this could be a great romantic adventure and experience for both of you! BUT, if you are on a family vacation it may come as a little bit of a surprise for everyone. I have found myself on one or two nude beaches for quite some time before I actually realized where I was! My favorite beaches to go to for family time would be 'Big Beach' on the Southside or if you go to the Northshore there is Baldwin Beach, very calm and spread out, and right in the town of Paia where you can score some awesome food!

10. HITCH-HIKING IS A THING HERE

When you are driving around the island you may see a large number of people hitch-hiking! Now back where you are from you most likely had it drilled in your head as a kid that hitchhiking is dangerous (understandably so) and to NEVER pick up hitch-hikers. However on the island this is a different story. Sometimes hitch-hiking is actually the means for transportation for a lot of people living there. You have to keep in mind you are on an island, and that many locals know each other so it is not nearly as "scary" as it sounds or you may be used to it. This being said if you are headed somewhere for the day and see someone hitch-hiking on the side of the road, feel free to pull over and give them a lift! If you are renting a truck of some sort you can let them hop in the back even, you can never get enough of that island breeze!

    I spent the first few months hitch-hiking around the island while I worked on saving for a vehicle, and can honestly say it was one of my greatest experiences while living there! I met so many locals that were so far beyond friendly. Hitch-hiking around allowed me to meet people, and get a feel for how friendly and helpful everyone really is there! I also got a lot of great advice for being a "first-time islander" and great suggestions on hikes to go on and waterfalls to go check out! I was honestly astonished at first how friendly people were to me, being a stranger, and how open they were to telling me about the great spots to go to on the island! I always expected that the best hikes and beaches to check out would be something that the locals would keep on the 'down low' to avoid too much traffic going to their favorite spots. This is something I would totally

>TOURIST

understand with how many visitors come to the island on a daily basis (THOUSANDS per day) however It seemed though that everyone was so friendly and wanted to share the beauty of their home with you, and all they ask in return is to treat the land with respect, which is something I hope everyone would do regardless!

One of my best experiences I had in Maui was actually when I was hitch-hiking with my best friend, it was the third day of being in the Island, and we were picked up by an older woman named Ursula. She sat and talked about how she grew up there and about all of her beautiful children and how much she loved them. She was easily the kindest woman I have ever met in my entire life. This woman was so kind hearted, I kid you not, I watched her swerve FOR A BUTTERFLY. A butterfly, I am not joking. At that moment, many people would have laughed it off, but for me it opened my eyes as to how genuine people there actually are. By the end of the ride she had us both smiling from ear to ear, gave us twenty dollars and said "go get some lunch you two girls must be starved!" (typical momma!) and off we went. To this day that experience makes me smile.

11. CONSTANTLY CHECK THE WEATHER

This goes without saying, and this is where the phrase 'Island Weather' comes from. Being an island you have nothing but ocean winds surrounding you so a storm can roll in fairly quick. There have been numerous times I left my house to go on a hike (7 minute drive) on a beautiful sunny day, and by the time I got there, it was raining. If you want to download a local weather app and track that throughout your stay, you will be on top of anything that may come your way.

I am serious when I say a beautiful sunny day can disappear in moments. I liked to camp on the beach as much as I could when I got there, because why not?! I wanted to experience the island in every way, and as much as possible. We were camping in a tent just off the beach in the trees and we had heard the wind pick up early in the morning, but did not pay much attention to it. We are right on the ocean, there is going to be wind right? Well then suddenly our tent actually started to feel like it was going to blow over, so I popped my head out of my tent and realized we were in the middle of a full blown island storm. We

>TOURIST

rushed and grabbed all of our things and hopped out of the tent, and there were trees flying all around us, branches breaking, the whole nine yards. Needless to say we started running back to town to find shelter before the rain started to come. One miraculous thing I noticed that I found so fascinating about nature there, was that while we were leaving the beach area you could see what almost looked like giant groups of bugs fleeting away from the shore. It was like their instincts had kicked in and they knew there was a storm coming. It was something pretty small, but rather fascinating. So keep that in mind, that a storm can blow in within minutes. If you are somewhere far away from your vehicle, just pack a nice raincoat or jacket in your hiking pack.

12. EVERY PART OF THE ISLAND HAS A SLIGHTLY DIFFERENT WEATHER PATTERN

In addition to checking the weather, be aware of what section of the island you are planning on visiting that day so you can plan an adventurous hike on the eastern side of the island, or a nice day at the beach on the southside. Each side of the island has a slightly different weather pattern that you should be aware of, even the middle of the island!

The northshore I always referred to as the neutral zone, because it seems like it has a little bit of everything. The west side of the island where Lahaina is (the largest city on Maui) can be much hotter and drier than other parts of the island. I think that being the largest city on the island and the most populated, all of the traffic flow, such as people and vehicles, plays a huge role in why it is so much hotter. The southside of the island is very warm, doesn't get too much precipitation and is a wonderful area to spot some outstanding sunsets! Some of the most beautiful beaches on the island are on the southern side, which is also where you will find the majority of the large 'fancier' resorts. (Four Seasons, etc.) The eastern side of the island is where the infamous jungle lies. It gets the majority of the precipitation for the island which is why it is so green and lush, and this is also where you will find Hana. If you are going to the eastern side of the island, regardless of how it looks outside or what the weather may say on your phone, I suggest packing a jacket or raincoat. Lastly, there is the middle of the island which was always my favorite. It is referred to as "Upcountry". This is where you may actually come across needing a sweater or jacket because it can reach the low 40's at night-time! "Upcountry" always held a special place in my heart because even if you are a sun nut like myself and want to spend the rest of your life being warm and wearing shorts, escaping to a little higher elevation where you can feel crispy, fresh, chilly air and be able to wear a sweater can be something special. This part of the island can also be rather significant since it is above sea level, you can find some great areas to look down and see the ocean. If you happen to be in the right place at the right time, you may even catch a double or triple rainbow! (Yes triple rainbows are a thing!)

13. BRING WARM CLOTHES

Traveling to Maui everyone thinks that they will only need shorts, tank tops, and a bikini. Which may be true if you plan on only visiting the beaches there. If you plan on completely experiencing the island though (and hopefully did you research on what you plan on doing!) I would suggest bringing some warm clothes or at least a jacket. There are some fun activities that may get a little chilly because the island has a very diverse array of weather patterns (like explained above).

Visiting the volcano crater definitely will permit even a coat and some warm blankets to snuggle up in as you watch the sunrise. If you plan on going ziplining you may want to bring a light jacket, depending on where you zipline because some can get a bit of a chill when you get going. Shoes are a good thing to bring as well in case a night gets rather chilly, but WATER SHOES are a big suggestion of mine. All of this is also dependent on what time of year you plan on visiting, because of the change in season this will depict on what you should pack.

14. PICK THE RIGHT TIME OF YEAR TO TRAVEL

Maui's "Tourist Season" is winter-time on the mainland, understandably as who wouldn't want to bask in the sunshine when your friends back home are getting pummeled with snow!? But because this is what Maui refers to as " Tourist Season" expect everything to be a little busier on the island.. but don't worry, Maui prepares for it! I add this tip here

>TOURIST

because one little detail that is commonly by-passed or forgotton is when "the surf is up". What this means is it is basically surf season. That is when the tide is extremely high but also can be extremely dangerous for anyone who is not familiar. When the tide is up there can be as big as 30 ft' wells just at the shoreline, and the infamous "Jaws" can reach 70 ft' wells! Now if you are inexperienced and try to jump in with a boogie board you are almost guaranteed to be sucked in and can get seriously injured, I don't particularly see this happening because once you see how big the waves are on the shore you will know that you cannot just jump in. So choose the best time of year for your stay. Summer was always my favorite because it gets the warmest, there are not very many tourists on the island and the ocean is at its calmest. Now if you specifically wanted to try surfing for the first time then basically any other time besides winter would work perfect, even in the summer. The waves fluctuate around the island so if the west side is not getting any waves, the north shore could be getting great little ones for beginning surfers. Choosing the right time of year is simply dependent on WHAT exactly you are looking to do for your stay.

15. FIND THE RIGHT LUAU

There is a shmorgishborg of Luaus all over the island of all different types and tastes depending on what you are looking for. There are many that are coordinated directly through the resort you may be staying at even. There are types that can pertain to your family or a romantic stay with your partner. Who doesn't want to see hula dancing and fire spinning when you go to Hawaii? That's what you picture when you think of Hawaii right?! Well there is so much more to it than you can ever imagine. Luaus are magical because they show you truly how passionate the Hawaiians are about their culture and how open they are to sharing it, so finding the right one for you and your family will make your experience that much more memorable. I suggest finding one not performed directly out of a resort. I also suggest going to a Luau on your first night on the Island because they can be pretty spendy to attend one, and finding the right one will definitely pay off!

>TOURIST

16. CONSIDER PACKING YOUR OWN SNORKEL GEAR

This is a little hidden gem I learned from living there and realizing that renting snorkel gear is SO EXPENSIVE! Don't get me wrong I am all for supporting locals, which I encourage! But, if you are trying to experience Maui without breaking the bank, I suggest buying a cheap pair of snorkel gear and packing it with you, this way too you are not limited to only going once! You can go as much as you have time to while you are visiting. When you break it down, the little extra space in your bag will not even compare to the amount of money you will save on rental costs, especially if you got more than once.

17. FOOTWEAR

BUY WATER SLIPPERS! You will not regret it! One thing I wish I would have brought with me were water slippers. Having them would have greatly saved my poor little toes and feet from the wreckage I experienced living there. I am not sure how you may be, but I am not the most coordinated when it comes to walking or avoiding stubbing my toe on things. I do not know why it took me so long to purchase a pair either... I hurt my feet within probably the first few days of living there, but for some reason it took me months to buy a pair!

I cannot tell you how many times I was strolling down the beach looking at the stars and I stubbed my toe on a large piece of coral that was hiding in the sand. And if you are not familiar with coral, it is very rough and gritty. So if you stub a toe, it is more often than not going to break the skin. There are also large chunks of coral that hide in the sand along the shoreline and in the water so walking into the water you can easily stub a toe on a piece of coral. So to protect your feet I suggest buying a pair of water shoes. You do not have to purchase an expensive pair, any cheap pair will do the trick. They will also come in handy if you want to do any waterfall jumping too because hitting your feet too hard on the water if you land wrong can be a tad painful.

Now getting little cuts on your feet here and there may not be the biggest deal to many people. It is not so much receiving the cut, as it is the hassle of taking care of it. When you get a cut on your feet, trying to put a band-aid on it to avoid infection simply just doesn't work because once you get back in the ocean,

>TOURIST

that band-aid is coming off. "Yuck!" No one wanted to see a band-aid floating in the water! So then you are stressed to keep it clean and covered, but also still enjoy the ocean waters. You can let it do it's thing, but the one thing to keep in mind in Maui is that because of the warm weather, infections can actually fester rather than heal naturally like you may do back home.

Unfortunately, on the island there is a high risk of getting staph infection in a minor cut (especially on your feet) because sand is an nact for hiding bacteria. So when you receive a cut on an area that is almost impossible to keep sand out of, it will get infected. This comes across as quite scary to many people because staff can be serious if untreated, but you just have to take the right precautions. If you do happen to get a cut just keep it clean and wash the sand out of it immediately when you are done in the ocean. As long as you do not let sand remain in a cut, you have nothing to worry about. BUT, having a pair of water shoes can help you avoid this headache altogether.

18. PACK A FIRST AID KIT

This one actually deserves a spot in the top three because it is very important. You never know where you will be when you may (stub a toe on coral per say...) and need some antibiotic ointment and a nice waterproof bandaid! This won't be a huge damper on your vacation if you do not have one. But I will say it will make your life much easier, especially with little kiddos because you know if they get one boo-boo, that is all you will hear until you get back to your hotel and deal with it. There can also sometimes be thorns on certain plants or flowers that may snag you, but nothing a first aid kit won't fix! Having one on hand to keep in the car or your backpack can save a lot of stress.

>TOURIST
19. PLANT LIFE

There are plants on the island that are native, and some planted by man, many years ago. Luckily the Hawaiian Islands do not contain a large number of exotic plants that are poisonous that should cause worry to you or your family. When arriving on the Island pick up a Hawaiian Plant Identification Guide/ Brochure that contains pictures and descriptions of such plants. Pictures always help and then you have an easy reference to carry around during your hikes! These brochures are at every airport and hotel so it will be easy to find one. There is one plant called 'Long-thorn Kiawe', and you will find this tree planted along many beach coastlines. The specific tree got its name for the very long and very hard thorns on the branches that fall to the ground so be careful walking barefoot if you see fallen branches because they do not feel good to step on, and are very difficult to get out! I specifically speak of this tree because it is known for causing stress in locals' lives. Kiawe is not native to the island so it is not really a favored plant. Getting a thorn stuck in your foot is like a splinter times ten and can also get infected easily as it is an open wound. So watch where you are walking if you are barefoot!

20. LOCK YOUR CAR DOORS

Maui is a magical place to visit but just like any other place, there should be caution for theft. Due to this being a high tourist location and many travelers have at least one valuable item on them whether it be a go-pro or just a cell phone or simply your wallet, tourists vehicles are often targeted for theft. But do not worry this does not mean it is an unsafe place to visit whatsoever. This is easy to avoid as all rental cars have a good locking system. Just remember to keep any valuables out of sight in your vehicle, or leave them behind if at all possible and lock your doors anytime you are away. I suggest opting for a go-pro over an expensive camera for your vacation!

21. FIND A GOOD PAIR OF SHADES

One thing I did before moving to Maui that was a game-changer was finding a good pair of shades! This is a no-brainer but with all of the other packing it can be easily forgotten, and just like forgetting a bikini you could find yourself dropping some big bucks on a

>TOURIST

good pair of shades. I suggest getting a polarized pair with the contant sunshine you will be in. I bought a very inexpensive polarized pair and I still have them to this day, 5 years later. Definitely an essential item!

22. DO NOT TOUCH THE SEA TURTLES

When you are thinking about visiting Maui, I am sure swimming with the sea turtles crossed your mind. They truly are magnificent creatures, but sadly they are still on the endangered species list. If you happen to be swimming in the ocean and find one bobbing up next to you, do not panic, they are harmless. But do not overcrowd them! During sunrise and sunset sea turtles love coming onto the beach and sunbathing. However if you do come across one lounging in the sand, please leave them be. They can become vulnerable to harmful bacteria through human contact, leaving them susceptible to disease. This also goes for corals, rays, and smaller species of sharks if you happen to encounter one on a scuba trip. Feeding or touching of sea turtles is considered a disturbance but now actually illegal on most islands, Maui included.

23. NOT ALL RESIDENTS ARE "HAWAIIAN"

This is a very good tip to know before visiting to avoid offending anyone. Today, only about 10% of the residents in Hawaii are ACTUALLY 'hawaiian'. There is a hawaiian island called 'Niihau' or "the forbidden island" because non-native Hawaiians are restricted to go there. Many of the residents of the hawaiian islands are actually of polynesian descent, and can be easily confused as being 'hawaiian'. Matter of fact, many true hawaiians are not actually seen on the high tourist islands or highly visited areas of the island. Majority of the time they stay on the lesser visited parts of the island.

24. CHOOSE YOUR NEXT ISLAND FROM HERE

Many people are not aware that there are so many hawaiian islands. All Together there are 9 islands that make up "The Hawaiian Islands". (The Big Island, Maui, Oahu, Kahoolawe, Lanai, Molokai, Kauai, Niihau, and a very small one near Niihau called

>TOURIST

Kaala.) When someone says Hawaii, more often than not they are referring to 'The Big Island' because this is the largest island of the entire chain. However, Oahu is the most commonly visited, and has the largest population of all of them. Each island is actually quite different and has a different character to it. Depending on what you are looking for on a vacation depends on what Island you should choose! Look into each Island separately to pick what is best for you. There are four main ones that are commonly traveled to, Oahu, The Big Island, Maui, and Kauai. Once you are on Maui you can fly to the interisland for very cheap!

25. ISLAND TIME IS A REAL THING

Locals who have been living there for years have acclimated to what is known as 'Island Time' and despite common disbelief, this is a real thing! Locals have a very calm presence and honestly just go with the flow day to day. So if you find yourself frustrated in the grocery line because you may be in a hurry, and some locals in front of you are chatting, or you are stuck behind someone driving leisurely, take a moment and remember where you are. You are on vacation and there are no worries! Locals are very relaxed and friendly and honestly seem to never be in a hurry! Enjoy the environment!

26. DO NOT IGNORE WARNING SIGNS

There are all sorts of warning signs, from cliff edge caution signs to endangered plant species signs. READ THEM ALL! These signs are posted for your benefit and you should always read them to remain respectful to the land and those living there. There are also many signs posted near beaches, or in national parks that are full of incredible information about the land.

27. PICK THE RIGHT TIME OF YEAR TO TRAVEL

This is important to keep in mind, because one thing many travelers think about Hawaii is that it is just sunny and beautiful year-round. Which for the

>TOURIST

most part is true, but not completely because they still have seasons. During the winter time it can still be sunny and beautiful in Maui, BUT there can also be lots of rain. The eastern side of Maui actually gets the majority of their rain during this time of year which is essential for all the plant-life and farms out that way. This time of year is also when the surf is up and the ocean can be a bit intimidating and dangerous to swim in.

28. WHALE WATCHING IS NOT YEAR – ROUND

Maui is actually one of the best spots for whale watching in the world! During their annual winter migration, thousands of North Pacific Humpback whales pass through hawaiian waters and their route passes right past Maui. Your best chances of seeing whales are from a boat, but can also be sighted from certain beaches. The scenic McGregor Point lookout west of Maalaea and the beaches of Kaanapali, Kihei and Wailea are also great spots to see whales. One thing to keep in mind is this is not a year-round event! November through May is when they migrate and is your best bet at catching a view of them.

29. DON'T JUST STAY IN RESORT TOWNS

The resort towns are remarkable, honestly everywhere on the island is remarkable...but to truly catch the spirit of Maui I suggest you make your way to all the smaller towns. If you are unsure of where to explore, just drive around! You can drive around the entire island in a day (4 hours to be exact) and still have time to stop for food and take some pictures.

30. LEAVE THE CHICKENS ALONE

If you drive 'Upcountry' away from the beaches a little ways and come to the smaller local towns you will notice something. There are chickens walking around everywhere. On the sidewalks, in front of the doors of the supermarket, you name it. They are very friendly and more often than not will walk right up to you and take a snack out of your hand if offered. Be kind to these little creatures because they are friends to the locals and important to the overall environment and culture on the island. If you try to shoo them away, you will most likely get a concerned look, just ignore them and keep walking if you are not a fan.

31. LOCAL ARTISTS

This should be on your to-do list when arriving, because Maui has an enormously large amount of local artists all over the island! Many artists have their own shops that you can check out, but there is also a huge variety of street art! People sit and make beautiful hats out of palm leaves, wire wrap jewelry, whittling things out of wood, or will paint something on the spot for you! You will also find people just enjoying their life and playing melodies on their guitar or ukulele. It is one of my favorite things to check out all the art displayed in art halls or little window shops, but overall I absolutely adore supporting local artists and always carry cash on me to contribute to this wonderful trade!

32. CHECK OUT THE LOCAL ART GALLERIES

In addition to the street art, the local art galleries are a sight to see. They generally are very expensive pieces if looking to purchase one, but rightfully so. There are so many fascinating different types of art there, and talented people I would suggest checking out any art gallery you come across!

33. FIND A DRUM CIRCLE

There is something truly magical about sitting and listening to a drum circle. Many times I have seen one or two people start playing their hand drums and then within no time you have 10-15 people contributing to a drum circle and people dancing or even spinning fire! It is a very contagious event! The rhythm is impossible not to dance to or at least tap your foot to! If you are wanting to seek one out, every Sunday on the southside of the island there is a beach just off of "Big Beach" called " Little Beach" that has a drum circle at sunset and is one for the books. BUT, before embarking on this mission, you should know that

"Little Beach" is a nude beach, so this may be for a kid-free experience.

34. THE ROAD TO HANA

This is the number one activity tourists do when they come to Maui. The infamous 'Road to Hana' is breathtaking. It takes a little over an hour to get there with no stops because once you start to enter the jungle there are very windy roads and they are very narrow so you must stop and let cars coming the opposite way pass. So DO NOT SPEED AROUND THESE CORNERS. Also because these roads are so tight they are not friendly to those who may have car sickness, but do not worry most gas stations before you take the drive offer remedies for this. Pack your cameras for this trip though because there are stops along the way you do not want to miss!

35. BAMBOO FOREST

One of the best stops on the 'Road to Hana' is the bamboo forest in Haiku. There are plenty of pull off areas to park, hike around, take pictures and explore. If you are with a group of people I would suggest keeping within hearing range of each other because the bamboo has a knack for messing with your eyes. Because of the way bamboo grows so closely together it can be deceptive on how far or close people may be to you and you could very easily lose sight of someone. Long story short, you can very easily get lost in there! There are select trails to follow when entering the bamboo forest so stay on these and you should have no trouble!

36. DON'T MISS OUT ON HALEAKALA

Haleakala National Park is yet another one for the books! The infamous 'inactive' volcano crater! You want to check out Haleakala for sunset or sunrise (I suggest sunrise). The summit is 10,023 ft above sea level so this is when I suggest bringing a coat. Yes a coat, not a jacket, I would even suggest bringing blankets because at 4 o'clock in the morning it is brisk! There are numerous groups you can join that will go up together and show you around or you are

>TOURIST

welcome to do a solo mission with your family. There is however a fee to enter the park, so keep that in mind. This is a great chance to capture some amazing photography because being that high above sea level you can actually see The Big Island, Kaho'olawe, Lanai, Molokai and most of Maui.

37. GUIDED BIKE TOUR DOWN HALEAKALA

If you want to double up on excitement when checking out Haleakala, there are numerous companies that host a "bike down haleakala' event that is amazing! You meet somewhere near the bottom (usually one of the nearest beach parking lots) they supply you with a bike, and helmet with go-pro attachments and they drive you to the top. Once you are up there you will be led by a host and a group of you will bike down together, and usually through the town of Makaweo. This adrenal filled adventure is a must if you are an outdoorsy person!

38. DO NOT TAKE LAVA ROCKS

One more tip when checking out Halekala is to leave all lava rocks and natural items where they are. It is very tempting for many people (especially children) to take a little souvenir when departing the volcano crater but this is very frowned upon and will actually be taken from you if you are caught with one. Beyond the legality of this, there is actually an old wives tale stating that you will receive very bad luck if you take or even move any rocks from the crater, as there has been said that Haleakala has a very magical energy. Even the common activity of 'rock stacking' is usually a harmless and somewhat peaceful thing, but is very frowned up here.

39. FIND A ZIPLINE

There are three different companies that offer zipline tours, but I suggest checking out Piiholo Ranch. This one was always my favorite because the staff made it their number one goal to make sure you were smiling the entire time! Plus you are in the gorgeous 'upcountry' where it can be nice and cool in the afternoon and the ranch has a wonderful homey atmosphere.

40. VISIT THE LAHAINA BANYAN TREE

Lahaina is the largest town on the Island, and has some of the best restaurants and events to visit. One thing in particular it is known for is the large banyan tree that takes up an entire city block! Located at the corner of Front Street and Canal Street in Lahaina, this is actually the largest tree in Hawaii, just remember to be respectful and do not climb on it as this is taken as a huge disrespect.

41. BRING CASH BEFORE DEPARTING

This tip can be very handy, but very overlooked. There are not a lot of ATMs everywhere in Maui like there are in most towns and cities on the mainland. Also because the banks are different you will be looking at a hefty fee to pull cash out anywhere. I suggest bringing plenty of cash with you before departing to avoid throwing money away on atms fees.

42. NAKALELE POINT BLOWHOLE

There is one blowhole on the island of Maui. The best way to get to the Nakalele Blowhole is via West Maui's Kapalua. The drive is pretty easy, and there are some spectacular views! Head northeast past Kapalua on the Honoapiilani Highway (Hwy 30) for a short drive of about 15 or 20 minutes in total. There used to be an infamous naturally formed heart-shaped rock near the blowhole but unfortunately around January 2020 the rock naturally broke away and is now just half a heart. Now, this goes without saying to be extremely careful going near the blowhole, not just because of the blowhole itself, but the waves that crash around it. You can definitely get close to it though without being in harm's way.

>TOURIST

43. IAO VALLEY

This takes about 1-3 hours to hike the Iao Valley, and is one of my top suggestions on what hikes to take. It has so much culture in the history of how the valley was formed. When visiting Iao Valley, the same goes for almost anywhere on the Island, do not take anything. Most places in Maui are very sacred and nothing should be tampered with. One important tip when hiking this particular place is to STAY ON DESIGNATED TRAILS. It is very tempting to meander off and check out all that Iao Valley has to offer, but you will be slapped with a huge fine if you do!

44. WATCH OUT FOR CENTIPEDES

Everyone traveling to Maui always asks "Are there snakes there?" and I always respond "Well, no not exactly.." There are no snakes that live on any island of hawaii. However there are centipedes. Now these are not snakes at all, obviously they are insects. The centipedes in Maui can grow to be a foot long and an inch thick… yikes! There are also little ones. They have a pretty painful bite and can sometimes cause reactions depending on the person. They are usually a dark maroon color, but if you see one that is blueish, leave it alone because those ones are poisonous! They like to hang out in trees so be careful standing under a tree for too long because they can fall, and avoid brushy areas, this is generally where they are. But do not be too worried, it is not very common to get bitten by one, but is something to be aware of.

45. PACKAGE DEALS

Consider looking into a package deal if you want to explore ways to save money! Booking a package deal that includes some combination of airfare, accommodations, and rental car is usually the most cost-effective way for two people to travel to Maui. Pleasant Holidays, United Vacations, Hawaiian Airlines, and Air Canada Variations are some of the biggest and most comprehensive packages to Hawaiii. Be careful to read the fine print to avoid any additional fees, but this could be a great option for you.

>TOURIST

46. GROCERY BAGS

Maui has made plastic and styrofoam illegal, but paper bags are a great go to! If you want to be one step ahead and help with conservation, feel free to bring a reusable grocery bag, locals will be very appreciative! Do not feel obligated to do this, but refrain from asking for plastic bags, utensils, cups, etc.

47. BRING A LITTLE SOMETHING

If you are fortunate enough to befriend a local and be invited to their home-particularly for a meal, it is considered very good manners to bring a small gift of some kind. A bottle of wine, a light pupu (appetizer) or local treat, some fresh fruit from the farmer's market, or some flowers. It's the local way, just a little token showing appreciation for the invitation. This is sure to earn you a smile and a heartfelt "mahalo".

48. GRATUITIES

Hawaii is a U.S. state, so gratuities are expected in accordance with U.S. standards. For instance, 18-20% tips are the norm in restaurants. There are plenty of online sites that will give you the rundown on appropriate U.S. tipping procedures - which services warrant a tip, whom to tip, and how much. Please do not tip according to U.S. customs, not according to the country you are from. Not tipping (or vastly under tipping) your waiter or waitress is a sure way to earn that dreaded stink-eye as you're headed blissfully out the door.

49. TAKE YOUR SHOES OFF BEFORE ENTERING

It is customary when visiting a local's home to remove your shoes and leave them just outside the door. The telltale sign of a great party is a big ol' pile of shoes at the entryway! Some businesses, condos, and vacation homes might also ask you to honor this custom, and it is very polite for you to do so. (It is NOT polite to take someone else's shoes when you

>TOURIST

depart, so make sure you know which ones are yours!) Remove your shoes, even if you are unsure.

50. PACK IT IN PACK IT OUT

The island's environment, both on land and in the sea, is precious and fragile. Please respect it. Dispose of your trash properly. Don't leave cigarette butts - or anything else - in the beach sand (and remember that smoking is prohibited on all county beaches). Be cautious about removing any natural items as souvenirs. It is illegal to take sand (since 2013), dead coral, rocks and other "marine deposits" from the beach. (The exceptions are driftwood, shells, beach glass, and seaweed.) If we all take care of it, this beautiful environment will thrive and endure for many future generations to enjoy. Treat this precious island environment with care and respect.

>TOURIST
TOP REASONS TO BOOK THIS TRIP

Plant Life: There are some of the most fragrant and breathtaking flowers and plants that live here, by far one of my FAVORITE parts of the island is their plant life!

People: The people are very friendly and welcoming, you almost forget you are on vacation because you get lost in the abundance of bliss and serenity here.

Island Culture: A magnificent dive into the culture of the Hawaiian Islands that truly inspires your spirit.

>TOURIST
PACKING AND PLANNING TIPS

A Week before Leaving

- Arrange for someone to take care of pets and water plants.
- Email and Print important Documents.
- Get Visa and vaccines if needed.
- Check for travel warnings.
- Stop mail and newspaper.
- Notify Credit Card companies where you are going.
- Passports and photo identification is up to date.
- Pay bills.
- Copy important items and download travel Apps.
- Start collecting small bills for tips.
- Have post office hold mail while you are away.
- Check weather for the week.
- Car inspected, oil is changed, and tires have the correct pressure.
- Check airline luggage restrictions.
- Download Apps needed for your trip.

Right Before Leaving

- Contact bank and credit cards to tell them your location.
- Clean out refrigerator.
- Empty garbage cans.
- Lock windows.
- Make sure you have the proper identification with you.
- Bring cash for tips.
- Remember travel documents.
- Lock door behind you.
- Remember wallet.
- Unplug items in house and pack chargers.
- Change your thermostat settings.
- Charge electronics, and prepare camera memory cards.

\>TOURIST

READ OTHER GREATER THAN A TOURIST BOOKS

Greater Than a Tourist- California: 50 Travel Tips from Locals

Greater Than a Tourist- Salem Massachusetts USA 50 Travel Tips from a Local by Danielle Lasher

Greater Than a Tourist United States: 50 Travel Tips from Locals

Greater Than a Tourist- St. Croix US Birgin Islands USA: 50 Travel Tips from a Local by Tracy Birdsall

Greater Than a Tourist- Montana: 50 Travel Tips from a Local by Laurie White

Children's Book: Charlie the Cavalier Travels the World by Lisa Rusczyk Ed. D.

> TOURIST

Follow us on Instagram for beautiful travel images:
http://Instagram.com/GreaterThanATourist

Follow *Greater Than a Tourist* on Amazon.

CZYKPublishing.com

> TOURIST

At *Greater Than a Tourist*, we love to share travel tips with you. How did we do? What guidance do you have for how we can give you better advice for your next trip? Please send your feedback to GreaterThanaTourist@gmail.com as we continue to improve the series. We appreciate your constructive feedback. Thank you.

>TOURIST

METRIC CONVERSIONS

TEMPERATURE

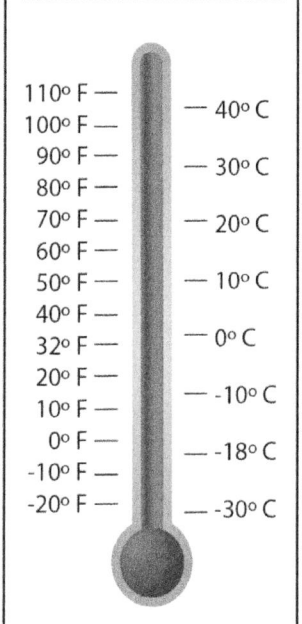

110° F — — 40° C
100° F —
90° F — — 30° C
80° F —
70° F — — 20° C
60° F —
50° F — — 10° C
40° F —
32° F — — 0° C
20° F —
10° F — — -10° C
0° F —
-10° F — — -18° C
-20° F — — -30° C

To convert F to C:

Subtract 32, and then multiply by 5/9 or .5555.

To Convert C to F:
Multiply by 1.8
and then add 32.

32F = 0C

LIQUID VOLUME

To Convert:................Multiply by
U.S. Gallons to Liters................. 3.8
U.S. Liters to Gallons 26
Imperial Gallons to U.S. Gallons 1.2
Imperial Gallons to Liters....... 4.55
Liters to Imperial Gallons 22
1 Liter = .26 U.S. Gallon
1 U.S. Gallon = 3.8 Liters

DISTANCE

To convert ....Multiply by
Inches to Centimeters 2.54
Centimeters to Inches 39
Feet to Meters....................... .3
Meters to Feet 3.28
Yards to Meters 91
Meters to Yards 1.09
Miles to Kilometers 1.61
Kilometers to Miles............ .62
1 Mile = 1.6 km
1 km = .62 Miles

WEIGHT

1 Ounce = .28 Grams
1 Pound = .4555 Kilograms
1 Gram = .04 Ounce
1 Kilogram = 2.2 Pounds

>TOURIST
TRAVEL QUESTIONS

- Do you bring presents home to family or friends after a vacation?
- Do you get motion sick?
- Do you have a favorite billboard?
- Do you know what to do if there is a flat tire?
- Do you like a sun roof open?
- Do you like to eat in the car?
- Do you like to wear sun glasses in the car?
- Do you like toppings on your ice cream?
- Do you use public bathrooms?
- Did you bring a cell phone and does it have power?
- Do you have a form of identification with you?
- Have you ever been pulled over by a cop?
- Have you ever given money to a stranger on a road trip?
- Have you ever taken a road trip with animals?
- Have you ever gone on a vacation alone?
- Have you ever run out of gas?

- If you could move to any place in the world, where would it be?

- If you could travel anywhere in the world, where would you travel?

- If you could travel in any vehicle, which one would it be?

- If you had three things to wish for from a magic genie, what would they be?

- If you have a driver's license, how many times did it take you to pass the test?

- What are you the most afraid of on vacation?

- What do you want to get away from the most when you are on vacation?

- What foods smell bad to you?

- What item do you bring on ever trip with you away from home?

- What makes you sleepy?

- What song would you love to hear on the radio when you're cruising on the highway?

- What travel job would you want the least?

- What will you miss most while you are away from home?

- What is something you always wanted to try?

>TOURIST

- What is the best road side attraction that you ever saw?
- What is the farthest distance you ever biked?
- What is the farthest distance you ever walked?
- What is the weirdest thing you needed to buy while on vacation?
- What is your favorite candy?
- What is your favorite color car?
- What is your favorite family vacation?
- What is your favorite food?
- What is your favorite gas station drink or food?
- What is your favorite license plate design?
- What is your favorite restaurant?
- What is your favorite smell?
- What is your favorite song?
- What is your favorite sound that nature makes?
- What is your favorite thing to bring home from a vacation?
- What is your favorite vacation with friends?
- What is your favorite way to relax?
- Where is the farthest place you ever traveled in a car?

- Where is the farthest place you ever went North, South, East and West?
- Where is your favorite place in the world?
- Who is your favorite singer?
- Who taught you how to drive?
- Who will you miss the most while you are away?
- Who if the first person you will contact when you get to your destination?
- Who brought you on your first vacation?
- Who likes to travel the most in your life?
- Would you rather be hot or cold?
- Would you rather drive above, below, or at the speed limited?
- Would you rather drive on a highway or a back road?
- Would you rather go on a train or a boat?
- Would you rather go to the beach or the woods?

>TOURIST

TRAVEL BUCKET LIST

1.

2.

3.

4.

5.

6.

7.

8.

9.

10.

>TOURIST

NOTES

Printed in Great Britain
by Amazon